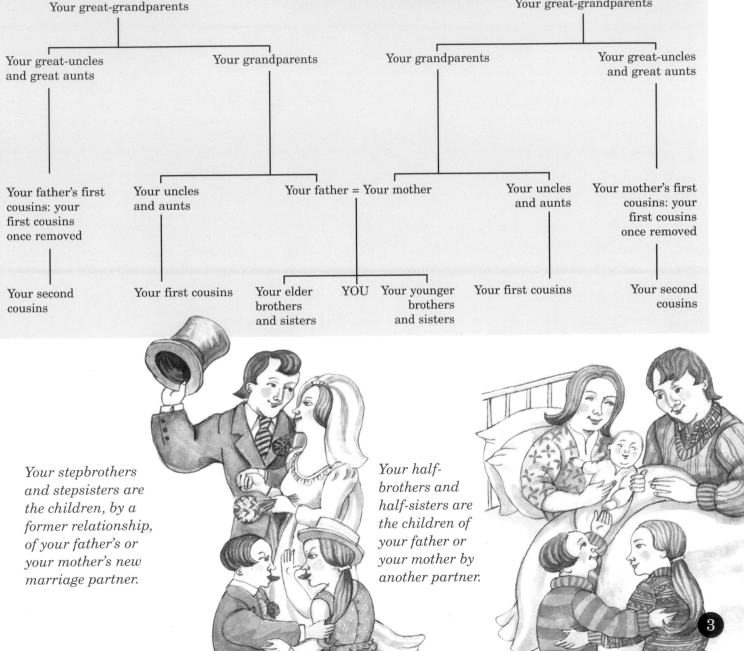

YOUR FATHER'S SIDE   **YOUR MOTHER'S SIDE**

Your great-grandparents   Your great-grandparents

Your great-uncles and great aunts   Your grandparents   Your grandparents   Your great-uncles and great aunts

Your father's first cousins: your first cousins once removed   Your uncles and aunts   Your father = Your mother   Your uncles and aunts   Your mother's first cousins: your first cousins once removed

Your second cousins   Your first cousins   Your elder brothers and sisters   YOU   Your younger brothers and sisters   Your first cousins   Your second cousins

Your stepbrothers and stepsisters are the children, by a former relationship, of your father's or your mother's new marriage partner.

Your half-brothers and half-sisters are the children of your father or your mother by another partner.

3

HIGHLAND LIFE

Highlanders wove tartan from wool brightly-coloured with vegetable dyes. The plaid was an enormous, midge-proof blanket, about 2 ½ metres wide and five metres long. To get into it, you laid it on the ground and pleated the centre part lengthwise. Then you lay down on it, gathered the bottom part around your waist, and secured it with a belt. There were several ways of draping the top half round your body. At night the plaid served as a sleeping bag.

currac, a triangle of linen worn by married women, fastened with silk cords or gold or silver pins

brooch

bonnet

clan plant badge

The Well-Dressed Highlander and His Wife

long linen shirt

short jacket

sporran, in which to keep valuables and, on active service, the daily ration of oatmeal

tartan plaid

garters, one metre long, tied on the outside with a special knot

tartan stockings

staff

buckled shoes

arisaid, a checked plaid with a white background

4

Out of doors, especially on the damp moors, both men and women went bare-legged and wore brogues. These were

light, deerskin shoes; the tops were punched with holes to let out water.

When armed, a Highlander carried: targe (shield), dirk (sometimes with his knife and fork in the sheath), sword, pair of pistols, powder horn, containing gunpowder to fire the pistols.

Here is a description of a house in the Highlands, written in about 1725. 'My landlady sat by a peat fire, in the middle of the hut; over the fireplace was a small hole in the roof for a chimney. The floor was common earth. The skeleton of the hut was formed of small crooked timber, but the beam of the roof was large out of all proportion. This is to render the weight of the whole more fit to resist the violent flurries of wind; for the whole fabric was set upon the surface of the ground like a table. The walls were about four feet high, lined with sticks wattled like a hurdle, built on the outside with turf; and thinner slices of the same served for tiling. When the hut had been built some time it is covered with weeds and grass; I have seen sheep, that got up from the foot of an adjoining hill, feeding upon the top of the house.'

From this description, make a drawing of the house. (Include some Highlanders, so that the scale of your drawing will be clear.) Or make a model of the house, from twigs, sticks, drinking straws; plasticine or clay; rough cloth like tweed or canvas for turf (or grass or grass clippings). For the sheep: pipe cleaners or match sticks, cotton wool, black felt pen. ('Wattled' means made of sticks or poles interwoven crosswise with twigs.)

Bonnie Dundee

In March 1689 a parliament met in Edinburgh to consider letters from both William and James VII asking for support. After the letters had been read out aloud, even some of the Jacobite members realised that James's cause was hopeless and that William would be declared King of Scotland as well as of England.

Not so John Graham of Claverhouse, Viscount Dundee, whom James had appointed as his general in Scotland. He stormed out of the chamber, and led his troop of cavalry out of the courtyard of Parliament House. They went through the Netherbow Port, and turned left along Leith Wynd and out into the suburbs below Calton Hill. They then rode along the shore of the North Loch, and halted at the Castle rock. The Castle, commanded by the Catholic Duke of Gordon, was under siege from the supporters of William. Dundee climbed up the west face to speak to Gordon and encourage him to hold out as long as he could.

Then Dundee rode out into the Highlands, to raise an army of the clans to fight for James against the Government.

One by one a number of clans rallied to him, and he trained them to adapt their fighting tactics to modern warfare. He ate with the men, and slept alongside them on the ground. He was their hero, even when he would not let them take plunder.

Here is an old map of Edinburgh. Starting at Parliament House, follow Dundee's route on a modern map of the city or by walking it (you will have to allow for the railway). Where was the Netherbow Port (its outline is marked by brass plates in the road)? The North Loch does not exist any more. What is there now? The street beside it, along which Dundee rode to the Castle, was then a country lane. What is its name today?

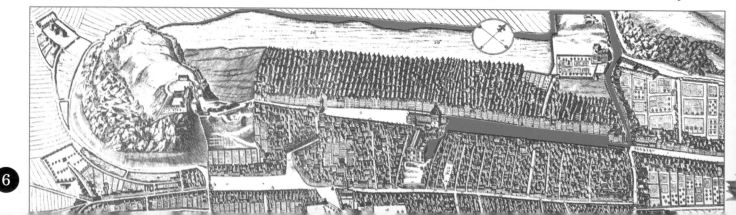

The Government of William and Mary sent General MacKay with the best available troops to fight against the Jacobite army. Dundee was in Lochaber in the west when he heard that MacKay was advancing to take Blair Castle. Whoever held the Castle controlled the main route to the north, through the long, narrow Pass of Killiecrankie.

Dundee was not ready, but with a forced march he managed to reach Blair Castle first. MacKay, with three thousand trained infantry, was already entering the Pass. Dundee had only two thousand Highlanders, tired and hungry after their march. Many of them had never fought in a proper battle. He knew that four thousand more men would join him within the next three days.

It was too late to organise an attack on the Pass itself. Dundee's choices were:
a) to wait for the other clans to arrive, and then pursue MacKay with superiority of numbers;
b) to march the six kilometres to the end of the Pass and wait for the Government army there.

What would you have done if you had been Dundee? When you have made your choice, turn over the page to see what he decided to do.

The chiefs sent out the fiery cross as a sign that the clans should gather.

THE BATTLE OF KILLIECRANKIE 27 JULY 1689

Encouraged by the fighting words of his council of war, Dundee led his army over the hills behind Blair Castle, and round to a hillside overlooking the exit to the Pass.

As the Government soldiers came out of the Pass, they saw some Highlanders high up to their right. MacKay gave orders to right turn and advance up the hill. At the top of a rise, the ground flattened out; beyond was a further rise.

On the second rise was the whole Jacobite army, drawn up clan by clan in battle formation. In the line, with his small band of faithful horsemen, was Dundee, who had been persuaded to change his red coat for one of yellow-brown, so that he would be less conspicuous.

For two hours, while MacKay organised his soldiers as best he could on the level space, and the sun dropped slowly towards the top of the hill on the other side of the valley, Dundee kept his wild Highlanders in check. Then, when the sun was no longer shining in their faces, he gave the order to charge.

The Government soldiers fired their muskets as soon as the Highlanders were within range and then struggled to fit bayonets into the muzzles. The Highlanders waited to fire until they were so close that they could not miss;

then they threw away their muskets and drew their swords. The Government line disintegrated. The fight was all over in three minutes.

MacKay had lost the battle, but not the war. At the very moment of victory, Dundee was killed by a stray bullet. Without him to lead them, the clans were defeated shortly afterwards in a street battle in Dunkeld. The first Jacobite rising had collapsed.

Yet Jacobite feelings continued, especially as William was proving to be an unpopular King. Members of some clans, especially in north-east Scotland and in the western Highlands, were Catholics. Many clan chiefs still regarded James VII as their King. William preferred to send his army to fight a war in France than to secure his position in Scotland.

n battle Highlanders discarded their plaids
nd fought in their waistcoats and shirts, tying
he tails in a knot between their legs.

THE MASTER OF STAIR DICTATES TO HIS SECRETARY

TO THE CLAN CHIEFS OF
SCOTLAND

HIS MAJESTY PROMISES THAT
NO FURTHER ACTION WILL BE
TAKEN AGAINST THE MEMBERS OF
ANY JACOBITE CLAN WHOSE
CHIEF SWEARS ALLEGIANCE TO
HIM AS THE TRUE KING
OF SCOTLAND
BEFORE 1 JANUARY
1692.

Some other way had to be found to subdue the
Highlands, perhaps by making an example of
one branch of a clan. In London, Sir John
Dalrymple, known as the Master of Stair, who
was William's Secretary of State for Scotland,
was devising just such a plot . . .

'Bobbing John' and the 1715 Rebellion

After the death of Queen Mary in 1694, William ruled alone. He died in 1702 after being thrown from his horse when it stumbled on a mole-hill. Jacobites drank toasts to 'the little gentleman in black velvet': the mole who made that mole-hill. William was succeeded by Queen Anne. What relation was she to him? Look it up in the royal family tree.

Queen Anne had no children who survived. The English Parliament had already decided that, after her, the throne should go not to James Edward Stuart, her half-brother, but to George, her second cousin, ruler of the Electorate of Hanover, in Germany. As the Scots were not even consulted about this, many of them felt they were not bound by the decision.

So when George I came to the throne even some Scots who had previously supported the Government had become disillusioned. Among them was the Earl of Mar, who was nicknamed 'Bobbing John'. He had worked hard for the Act of Union in 1707, when the Scottish and English parliaments were combined, in London. George not only dismissed him from his post as Secretary of State for Scotland, but then snubbed him at a party.

In September 1715, at the Braes of Mar, before six hundred Jacobite supporters, the Earl of Mar raised the standard of James VIII (James Edward Stuart). The gold ball at the top of the pole fell off, but he ignored this bad omen and gave a rousing speech.

Mar had the support of several of the Scottish nobility, as well as many, but not all, of the clans. By November he had an army of ten thousand men. Opposing him at Sheriffmuir on the Government side (now known as the Hanoverians) was the Duke of Argyll, with only four thousand men.

THE BATTLE OF SHERIFFMUIR, 13 NOVEMBER

It was an extraordinary battle, on a freezing day. The heathery moorland had so many humps and hollows that the two armies had difficulty finding each other. During the fighting the two commanders, each on his own right wing, could not see what was happening elsewhere.

When the fighting began, the infantry regiments on the Hanoverian left wing were still hurrying up the slope to the battlefield. The Highland clans on the Jacobite right wing made a furious charge and drove them back on to their own cavalry, causing great confusion. The retreat was sounded and the Hanoverian left wing fled back to Stirling. Mar and his Highlanders chased them as far as Dunblane. Meanwhile the Jacobite cavalry at the centre of the line sat and waited for orders.

The Jacobite left wing, which had no cavalry protection, was beaten right back in a half circle to the Allan Water by Argyll's cavalry, with the help of the disciplined fire of his infantry.

It was now dark. Each right wing had been victorious. The Jacobite survivors returned to Muthill, where they had camped the night before. The Hanoverians retired to Dunblane. In the morning both sides were prepared to renew the fighting. The Jacobites were so superior in numbers that they could hardly lose.

What happened next?
a) The Hanoverians won against all the odds?
b) The Jacobites won?
c) There was no result?
Turn to page 16 to see if you guessed right.

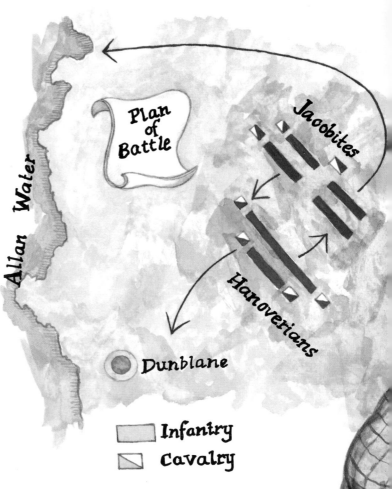

Allan Water

Plan of Battle

Jacobites

Hanoverians

⊙ Dunblane

☐ Infantry
◺ Cavalry

14

Feuds between clans were common. The most hated, because it was so powerful, was Clan Campbell. The Duke of Argyll was Chief, or MacCailein Mór, of Clan Campbell. On the right of the Jacobite front line were the MacLeans, sworn enemies of the Campbells, and the Macdonalds of Glengarry and of Glencoe. As the battle began, the Chief of the MacLeans shouted: 'This is a day we have longed for. There stands MacCailein Mór for King George. Here stands MacLean for King James. Charge, gentlemen!' The Highlanders behind him threw off their plaids, fired their muskets, and rushed forward with their claymores. When the Hanoverians fired back, and the Highlanders wavered, a Macdonald chief rallied them. Mindful that a Campbell commanded the troops who committed the Massacre of Glencoe, he cried: 'Revenge! Revenge! Today for revenge, and tomorrow for mourning!

THE RISING OF 1719

The Battle of Sheriffmuir ended in a 'no result'. When Argyll arrived on the battlefield on the second morning with his depleted army, there was no one there. Mar had decided not to fight. When James Edward Stuart landed in Scotland in December, hoping to claim his kingdom, his chance had gone.

The Jacobite cause was not completely lost. Spain was keen to damage the power of England. Cardinal Alberoni, the Spanish chief minister, found an ally in Sweden, who objected to George I taking for Hanover strategic territories which had once been Swedish. A plot was hatched between Alberoni and the Irish-born Duke of Ormonde who, like Mar, became a Jacobite after George I succeeded to the English throne. The King of Sweden promised arms and money. The King of Spain provided ships and five thousand troops. At the same time as an invasion of England, a small expedition would land in the west of Scotland and cause a diversion.

A storm scattered the invasion fleet, which never reached England. Though the Scottish expeditionary force landed and was joined by a thousand Highlanders, it was doomed. The Jacobite garrison at Eilean Donan Castle was blown up by a Government ship which had sailed into Loch Alsh. The Highlanders were defeated at Glenshiel largely by the skilful use of mortar fire.

That was the end of the 1719 rising. To try to prevent another one, the Government passed an act forbidding the carrying of arms, and ordered General Wade to subdue the Highlands. To make it easier to move troops around, between 1726 and 1740 Wade's soldiers built 390 km (243 miles) of all-weather roads and forty bridges.

Here is part of a letter written from Spain by the Duke of Ormonde in December 1718. It is in code.

Peter is James Edward Stuart. In the letter numbers are used instead of the names of people or countries. The missing names, in alphabetical order, are Alberoni; England; George I; King of Spain; King of Sweden; Scotland; James Edward Stuart. One of them appears twice. Can you break the code by filling in the names in their correct places?

To PETER . . .

14 CAME TO ME PRIVATELY AND INFORMED ME HE HAD INVITED 507 TO ENTER INTO AN ALLIANCE WITH 497, THE CHIEF PURPOSE OF WHICH WAS TO DETHRONE 249. HE ASKED ME WHAT I NEEDED TO MAKE AN ATTEMPT TO RESTORE 289. LATER HE PROMISED THAT 497 WOULD GIVE FIVE THOUSAND MEN FOR AN INVASION OF 165. I TOLD HIM IT WOULD BE NECESSARY TO HAVE A DIVERSION MADE IN 175.

Rob Roy MacGregor

Rob Roy MacGregor is one of the most famous of all Highlanders. He was on the Jacobite side at the Battle of Sheriffmuir, but arrived too late to fight. He may, though, have been acting as a special agent for the Earl of Mar, or for the Duke of Argyll, or as a double agent for both sides. In 1719 he survived the Jacobite defeat at Glenshiel; during the retreat he blew up a Government arms store.

He travelled hundreds of miles in Scotland and England to buy and sell cattle. It was common practice in the Highlands to steal cattle, as well as to breed them and deal in them. Rob had an extra way of making money. He invited rich landowners to pay him to protect their cattle from raiders. If they refused, he took their cattle himself.

As a Jacobite, Rob was hunted by Hanoverian troops. He was pursued by the Government for his cattle-rustling activities and for helping poor people who were in trouble with the law or behind with their rents. He was hounded by the Duke of Montrose, to whom he owed money, and sought by the Duke of Atholl, who wanted the reward for his capture.

He was caught several times, but always managed to escape. He finally died in his own bed. He was 63, a great age for someone in those days who spent most of his life out of doors in harsh weather, and who was for many years on the run.

In 1712 Montrose gave Rob £1000 (an enormous sum then) to buy cattle for him. Rob's chief drover absconded with the money, and disappeared. Rob offered to repay Montrose in instalments. The Duke, who was a spiteful man, wanted it all at once. When Rob could not pay, Montrose had him proclaimed an outlaw, and burned his house to the ground.

Rob Roy's most daring escape was in 1717. He was tricked into meeting the Duke of Atholl, who captured him and sent him under armed guard to Logierait Castle, the strongest prison in Perthshire. Three days later, having shared with his guards some whisky which he had had sent in to him, he slipped away on a horse brought by his servant, who had come pretending to seek a message for Rob's family.

The unfortunate Duke of Atholl had just written to General Carpenter, second-in-command of the Hanoverian in Scotland, praising himself for capturing Rob Roy, but now he had to write again.

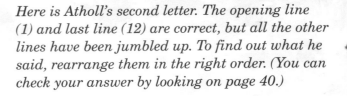

Here is Atholl's second letter. The opening line (1) and last line (12) are correct, but all the other lines have been jumbled up. To find out what he said, rearrange them in the right order. (You can check your answer by looking on page 40.)

1) About an hour after I wrote to you yesterday I

2) shall leave nothing untried that can be done

3) to sixty of my Highlanders to follow him

4) in the morning. I cannot say how vexed I am

5) to catch him, and I have already given orders

6) at Logierait yesterday, between 10 and 11

7) at this unlucky affair, but I assure you I

8) made his escape from the prison he was in

9) jailer prisoner, but nothing can retrieve this

10) had the misfortune to learn that Rob Roy had

11) wherever he can be found. I have made the

12) misfortune but capturing him.

THE ROB ROY GAME

For two players. You will need: a dice; two counters or small coins; six pieces of card, 7 cm by 8 cm.

Chance Cards

Write an instruction on each card:
1) Safe Conduct
2) Safe Conduct
3) You make a profit at a cattle sale. Have another go.
4) Cattle disease. Miss a throw.
5) Imprisoned in Logierait Castle. Play a safe conduct card or throw a 5 or 6 to escape.
6) Take refuge in Glen Shira. Play a safe conduct card or throw an even number to proceed.

Shuffle the cards and place them face downwards.

Rules

The winner is the first to arrive HOME by throwing the exact number.

Only one safe conduct card can be held at any time. You are not bound to play a safe conduct card that is in your possession, but if you do, you must play it before you throw the dice.

After the instructions on a chance card have been carried out or a safe conduct played, the card is put on a 'used' pile. When there are no cards in the chance pile, shuffle the 'used' pile and replace the cards face down.

HIGH WATER: Miss a throw
PASS OF ABERFOYLE / BALQUHIDDER: Beware ambush. Play a safe conduct card or throw a 2 or 3.

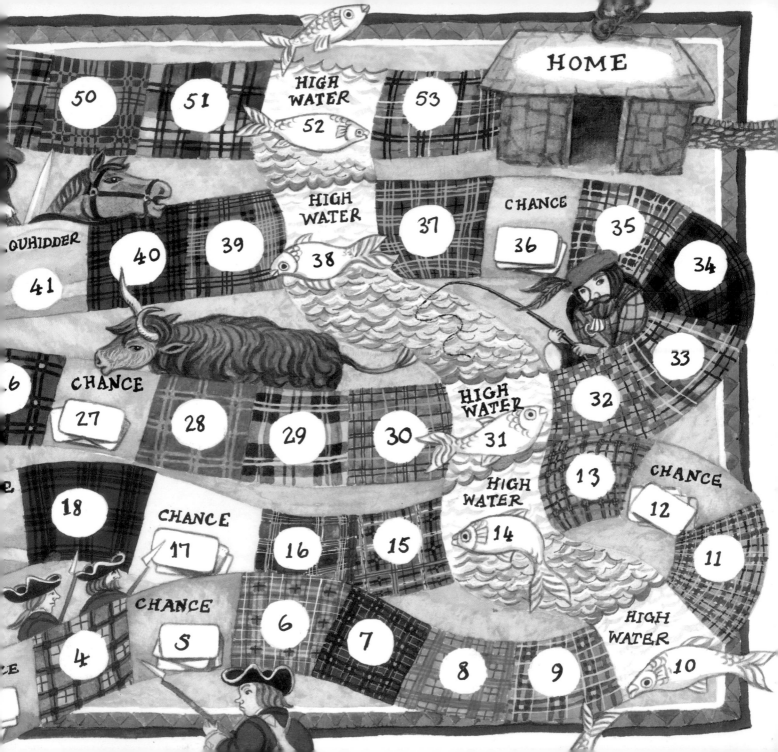

'Bonnie Prince Charlie'

On 23 July 1745, Charles, elder son of James Edward Stuart, landed on the tiny west coast island of Eriskay in disguise. Without telling his father, he had hired a French privateer and seven hundred troops, and bought arms and ammunition. A frigate carried himself and twelve companions. When the privateer was intercepted by a British warship and so badly damaged that it had to turn back, he went on without it, to try and conquer Britain on his own.

Two days later, he was on the mainland. He immediately sent messages to clan chiefs who might support him. Some tried to persuade Charles that the enterprise was so mad that he should return to Paris. He is reported to have replied: 'In a few days, with the few friends I have, I will erect the royal standard, and proclaim to the people of Britain that Charles Stuart is come over to claim the crown of his

LONDON GAZETTE
4 AUGUST 1745

CHARLES STUART SENSATION
BOGUS PRINCE LANDS IN SCOTLAND
£30,000 REWARD

The Government has announced a reward of £30,000 for the capture of Charles Edward Stuart, who claims to be...

ancestors, to win it, or perish in the attempt: you may stay at home, if you prefer, and learn from the newspapers the fate of your prince.'

That brave speech settled it. On 19 August, at Glenfinnan, before a gathering of a thousand, the royal standard was raised, and Charles formally claimed for his father the thrones of Scotland, England, and Ireland. The great adventure had begun!

Here are the crests and mottos of clans which joined Bonnie Prince Charlie at the beginning of his campaign.

Design an appropriate crest and make up a suitable motto for your family.

Macdonald of Clanranald

Macdonald of Keppoch/Glencoe (Latin: By sea and land)

Macdonald of Glengarry (Gaelic war cry: The raven's rock)

Cameron of Lochiel (Gaelic: Unite)

Stewart of Appin (Scots: Whither will ye)

THE JACOBITE CAMPAIGN

Having sent messages to other clans to meet him on his way, Charles set out from Glenfinnan with his Highlanders to secure his father's kingdoms. At about the same time, General Cope, the Government's commander-in-chief in Scotland, set out to meet him from Stirling. Both sides used roads which had been constructed by General Wade to help subdue the Highlands.

Either they missed each other or Cope decided he would prefer not to fight. He headed for Inverness. The Jacobites marched on to Perth, where Charles made a triumphal entry into the city. He was now joined by Lord George Murray, a younger brother of the Duke of Atholl, and James Drummond, who had been created Duke of Perth by James Edward Stuart. They were appointed Charles's generals.

George II, who had succeeded his father as King in 1727, now began to appreciate the real danger. He ordered ten infantry regiments to be shipped home from Flanders.

With his army grown to nearly 2500, Charles continued his march towards Edinburgh, the capital city of Scotland. Cope hurriedly embarked his army into ships, to reach Edinburgh that way.

Charles got there first. From his camp three kilometres outside the city walls, he despatched orders to the Town Council to surrender. The Council sent several deputations to him by coach, hoping to prolong the discussions until Cope arrived. Eight hundred Highlanders under Cameron of Lochiel waited outside the Netherbow Port for orders to storm it. In the end they got in without a fight.

Cope prepared for battle at Prestonpans. On the morning of 20 September he drew up his forces facing the direction from which the Jacobite army would come. It was a bad error of judgement . . .

The Jacobites got into Edinburgh by a trick. The coach bringing the latest deputation back from Charles's camp dropped its passengers in the High Street and then continued its way to the Netherbow Port. When the gate was opened to allow the coach to proceed to its stables in the Canongate, the Highlanders rushed through it from the other side.

This is where the Jacobite and Hanoverian armies were between 19 August and 21 September 1745. Fill in the places and dates on an outline map of Scotland, using an atlas as a guide (some of the places are no longer on a main road). Then draw in separate colours the routes of the two armies. On what date were they nearest to each other in the Highlands, and how far from each other were they on that day?

JACOBITES	HANOVERIANS
Glenfinnan, 19 August	Stirling, 20 August
Corrieyairack Pass, 27 August	Crieff, 21 August
Dalwhinny, 29 August	Dalnacardoch, 25 August
Dalnacardoch, 30 August	Dalwhinny, 26 August
Blair Atholl, 31 August	Ruthven Barracks, 27 August
Dunkeld, 3 September	Inverness, 29 August
Perth, 4–11 September	Nairn, 4 September
Stirling, 14 September	Elgin, 5 September
Linlithgow, 15 September	Aberdeen, 11 September
Edinburgh, 17–20 September	Dunbar, 16–19 September
Prestonpans, 21 September	Prestonpans, 20 September

MASTER OF SCOTLAND

AM 20 September. *The battlefield that Cope chose had the sea on his right and a stretch of bog on his left.*

PM 20 September. *The Jacobites came from the south west and took up positions on the other side of the bog. Cope swung his army round to face them.*

Dawn, 21 September. *The Jacobites, having been secretly shown a way across the bog, crossed it silently during the night and arranged themselves in battle order. In the half-light, Cope mistook their front line for bushes.*

AM 21 September. *When Cope realised his error, it was too late. He was still reforming his lines when the Jacobites charged. The battle was over in five minutes.*

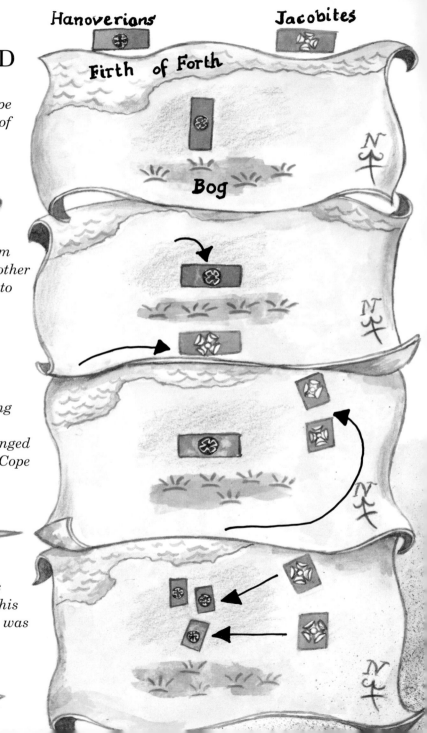

The Highlanders, some of whom were armed with scythes attached to poles, did terrible damage. Charles's military assistant wrote later: 'The field of battle presented a spectacle of horror, being covered with heads, legs, arms and mutilated bodies.' General Cope escaped the carnage and rode to Berwick, where it is said that he was sarcastically congratulated on being the first general to bring the news of his own defeat!

Charles was generous to his defeated opponents, providing carriages to take the wounded from the battlefield and surgeons to dress their wounds. He later released the Hanoverian officers he had captured on condition that they promised not to fight against him again.

After returning to Edinburgh Charles celebrated his triumph by dining in public at the Palace of Holyroodhouse, and giving concerts and balls. He was master of Scotland. Next on his list was the invasion of England.

THE INVASION OF ENGLAND

That the Jacobite army was able to march unopposed about 320 kilometres (200 miles) into England was due to luck as well as to good tactics. Though there was panic in London, and George II had loaded his personal valuables on board a yacht, ready to sail at a moment's notice, the luck could not last.

Hanoverian armies under General Wade and the Duke of Cumberland (son of George II) finally managed to discover the Jacobite route. A third army was lined up to protect London itself. Charles had told his supporters that they could expect English Jacobites to join them and that France was mounting an invasion of southern England. Neither of these things happened, if indeed they were ever more than fancies. At Derby he was persuaded to turn back. The long retreat began.

There was short-lived success at Falkirk, where a Hanoverian army was persuaded to attack uphill, in driving rain, against a storm-force wind. The retreat continued to Inverness, the last town in Scotland which was capable of being a Jacobite stronghold. Meanwhile the Duke of Cumberland, with the best available troops and artillery, had reached Aberdeen, where he trained his men to counter Highland fighting tactics. Confident in his own destiny, Charles prepared to do battle on the open moorland of Culloden. It was a disastrous mistake.

Inverness

Falkirk
Edinburgh

Glasgow

Carlisle

Manchester · GENERAL WADE

Derby

DUKE of CUMBERLAND

London

INVASION and RETREAT

We know exactly how many Highlanders Charles had with him when he stopped in Glasgow during his retreat from England. He ordered the Town Council to supply 12,000 shirts; 6000 coats and waistcoats; 6000 pairs of shoes and stockings; 6000 blue bonnets.

Finger Puppets
You will need: pencil, felt pens, thin card.

1. Make four rings of card 2 cm wide to go round your forefingers and middle fingers.
2. Make four small figures: either Jacobites (in kilts) or Hanoverians (the Hanoverian army wore red coats) or two of each.
3. Stick each figure to a ring.
4. Put the rings over your fingers. Move the puppets.
5. You might write a short play for them to act. For example, 'Bonnie Prince Charlie is persuaded to turn back at Derby'; 'The Duke of Cumberland discusses Highland fighting tactics with his officers'; 'Argument between two Jacobites and two Hanoverians'.

THE BATTLE OF CULLODEN, 16 APRIL 1746

The Jacobites were hungry and exhausted. Just one biscuit each had been issued during the previous 24 hours. When the battle began Charles had only five thousand men: the rest were asleep or out looking for food. Cumberland had nine thousand disciplined troops. A great number of his officers and men were Scottish: more Scots (including many Highlanders) fought against Bonnie Prince Charlie than for him during the 1745 Rebellion.

The Hanoverians, facing west, had the wind, snow, and hail at their backs. Their front line of eight infantry battalions, with two cavalry squadrons on the right, ran for 750 metres from the east end of a dry-stone wall. Behind were seven more battalions of foot, with two cavalry squadrons on their left. The Duke of Cumberland was immediately behind his front line and between the second and third infantry battalion on the right. Five artillery batteries, each of two 3-pounder guns, were in the spaces between front-line battalions.

The Jacobite front line of 12 detachments of Highland clansmen stretched from the west end of the wall, about 500 metres from the Hanoverian left. Its far end, which was outflanked by the Hanoverian right wing, was 750 metres from the enemy. The second line consisted of six infantry units. Charles was in the third line, with three units of infantry and one of cavalry. Three clusters of assorted artillery (13 guns in all), ahead and to the right, centre, and left of the front line, had little ammunition and were badly aimed.

The Jacobite cannons began the battle. The Hanoverian artillery replied with devastating effect, driving great holes in the Jacobite lines as they stood, waiting for orders. The Jacobite charge, when it came, was chaotic. The centre went out ahead, followed by the right. The clans on the left, either because they were sulking at not being in the place of honour on the right, or because they never got the order, went last. Cumberland ordered the infantry company on the left of his second line to a position ahead of and at right angles to the front line, with its backs to the wall.

From there it poured musket fire into the charging clansmen from the side.

The Jacobite centre and right bunched together. Though their charge took them through the three left-hand battalions, the Hanoverian second line stood firm. The Jacobite left, which had farther to go, turned back without reaching the enemy.

Before the Jacobite second line could be brought into the attack, the whole army was in flight, harried by the Hanoverian cavalry, which had ridden round behind the lines. Charles was led from the field, and went into hiding. The wounded Jacobites were butchered where they lay. Many of those who were caught as they tried to escape were slaughtered. The hunt was on for those who got away.

From the description, draw in a plan of the battle. You might use these symbols:

Make your own plan of the Battle of Culloden **N**

Redraw the outline of the wall on to a blank sheet of A4 paper, making the scale 1:50 (1 cm = 50 metres).

Artillery

Cavalry

Infantry

Prince Charles (white cockade)

Duke of Cumberland (black cockade)

Mark the movements of troops with arrows.

HUNT THE JACOBITE

How many Jacobites can you find in this picture? One of them is Bonnie Prince Charlie. Can you spot which he is?

There is an old story of a woman who lived near Culloden. When she heard of the Prince's defeat, she took her girdle (baking pan), oatmeal, and a jug of water down to the road, lit a fire, and baked for all she was worth. Each Highlander, as he ran past, heading for safety, took an oatcake from the pile.

To make your own oatcakes, add a large pinch of salt to 125 g (1 cup) of medium oatmeal and mix in 1 tablespoonful of melted dripping or oil. Knead into a ball with 125 g (1 cup) of boiling water, and roll out on a board dusted with oatmeal to $1/2$ cm thick. Cut into triangles and bake on both sides. (If you do not have a girdle, a heavy-based frying pan will do.)

Bonnie Prince Charlie

Flora Macdonald

THE ESCAPE OF THE PRINCE

The Hanoverians hunted Charles for five months until he was taken off the west coast of Scotland by a French ship. He remained only a few days in each place before moving on. At one point he sailed to the Outer Hebrides, returning to the mainland by way of the island of Skye. He always managed to keep just ahead of his pursuers, though one by one his guides were arrested soon after delivering him to the next place of safety. There was still a reward of £30,000 for his capture. No one ever betrayed him.

For two days Charles acted as the Irish maid of 23-year-old Flora Macdonald. She accompanied him from South Uist by boat to Skye, where she lived – 'Skye Boat Song' with its chorus, '. . . over the sea to Skye', remembers the journey. Soon after parting from him, Flora was arrested. She was imprisoned in the Tower of London for two years.

The rest of his story is much less romantic. He wandered from place to place in Europe. When he was 50, he was offered a large pension by the French to marry and produce an heir, to embarrass the British Government. The marriage was childless: his wife left him for a young Italian poet. Charles died in 1788, a drunken, fat old man.

There were many romantic Jacobite songs written after the '45 Rebellion. Here is part of one, by Lady Nairne.

Bonnie Charlie's now awa',
Safely o'er the friendly main;
Many a heart will break in twa,
Should he ne'er come back again.

Will ye no come back again?
Will ye no come back again?
Better loved ye cannot be,
Will ye no come back again?

English bribes were all in vain;
E'en though poorer we may be,
Silver cannot buy the heart
That ever beats for thine and thee.

Will ye no come back again, etc.

You might write some more verses of your own for this song.

After the '45 Rebellion

Besides hunting the leaders of the Rebellion, the Government needed to destroy the clan system to make sure that nothing like that ever happened again. An Act of Parliament in 1746 banned not only the carrying of arms but also the wearing of Highland dress.

Some chiefs who had supported the Rebellion had their lands confiscated. Others, who had spent all they had to help Bonnie Prince Charlie, had to sell their lands to sheep farmers from the south.

The land had for many years been unable to support the Highland way of life. As the population grew, more and more people emigrated. Many men joined the new Highland regiments which were raised to increase the fighting power of the British army abroad.

The Act against Highland dress was repealed in 1782, but by then weaving complicated tartans had become largely a forgotten craft. It had to be rediscovered.

No man or boy in Scotland shall wear or put on the clothes commonly called Highland clothes: the plaid, kilt, trowse, shoulder belts. No tartan or party-coloured plaid or stuff shall be used for coats. If any such person shall wear or put on the aforesaid garments or any part of them, every such person so offending shall suffer imprisonment during the space of six months, and being convicted for a second offence shall be liable to be transported to any of His Majesty's plantations beyond the seas for seven years.

Between 1763 and 1775 twenty thousand men, women, and children left the Highlands for north America alone. Among them were Flora Macdonald and her husband. They emigrated from Skye, where there was a dance called 'America', in which one by one the couples joined the whirling circle of dancers. This was said to represent the way in which emigration catches on, until it affects a whole neighbourhood.

Emigrants took with them place names from home. Look at the index to as large an atlas as you can find. How many places in the USA and Canada have the following names: Aberdeen, Campbell, Edinburg(h), Glasgow, Inverness, Lewis, Perth, Stewart? And where are they on the map?

Nova Scotia (New Scotland), now a province of Canada, was a Scottish colony from 1621 to 1632. Many Scots emigrated there later. Look at the map. Count how many Scottish place names there are in Nova Scotia today.

CLAN AND FAMILY TARTANS

Though the word 'tartan' is an ancient one, the idea of a clan or family having its own pattern of tartan is much more recent. Clan, in Gaelic, means 'children'. At the time of the '45 Rebellion there were no special clan tartans. Most of the earliest clan tartans are less than two hundred years old.

About 250 Scottish clans or families have their own special tartan or choice of tartans. You are also entitled to wear a clan tartan if you belong to a sept (branch) of that clan.

These tartans can be worn by anyone.

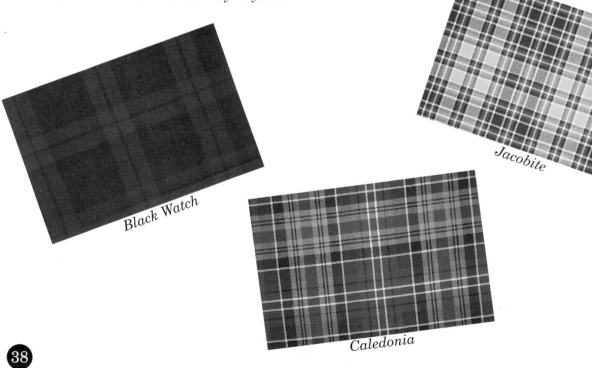

Hunting Stewart

Jacobite

Black Watch

Caledonia

To weave Tartan

You will need: a piece of stiff cardboard about 20 cm x 30 cm; three balls of wool in different colours; a bodkin or large darning needle, preferably with a blunt tip.

Ask an adult to help you cut the top and bottom of the cardboard as in the diagram.

Tie any colour of wool round the first pair of cuts. Wind it round in between the cuts until you are a third of the way along. Cut the wool and join on a second colour. Wind on for another third of the way. Join on and finish with the third colour. Secure the ends firmly. Cut lengths of wool in three colours, 6 cm wider than your card.

Thread the needle with a length of wool and weave through the vertical strands, passing over and under one, two, or three strands. Keep repeating this until you have used all your lengths or the card is full. Keep the woollen lengths close so that the effect is of woven cloth.

Experiment until you get a pattern that you like.

PLACES TO VISIT AND ANSWERS

Visitor Centres
Clan Donald Centre, Armadale, Skye
Culloden Moor, nr Inverness
Glenfinnan Monument
Pass of Killiecrankie, nr Pitlochry
Rob Roy and Trossachs, Callander
Skye Heritage Centre, Portree

Museums and Galleries
Glencoe and North Lorn Folk Museum, Glencoe
Highland Folk Museum, Kingussie
Inverness Museum and Art Gallery
National Museums of Scotland, Edinburgh
Scottish National Portrait Gallery, Edinburgh

Clan and Tartan Centres
Clan Cameron Museum, Achnacarry
Clan Donnachaidh Museum, Calvine
Clan Macpherson Museum, Newtonmore

Castles and Stately Homes
Abbotsford House, Melrose
Blair Castle, nr Pitlochry
Castle Fraser, Sauchen
Dunvegan Castle, Skye
Edinburgh Castle
Fort George, nr Nairn
Fyvie Castle, nr Turriff
Inveraray Castle
Palace of Holyroodhouse, Edinburgh
Traquair House, nr Peebles

Answers
Page 19: Duke of Atholl's letter
1, 10, 8, 6, 4, 7, 2, 5, 3, 11, 9, 12